M000306235

May the Lord give you a steadfast heart! Dan Schlueter Ps 57:7

Advantage
BOOKS

IN THE CRUCIBLE

DANIEL SCHLUETER

Dedication

To the one Jesus loves, my wife, my Chula, Lita!

I've watched Dan and Lita "walk their talk" with absolute integrity through our many years of friendship. Now they've given us their time capsule record of being transformed in the very crucible of one of life's most horrendous physical, spiritual, and relational challenges. What a gift their personal narrative has already been to me, a person so blessed in many ways, but one who over two decades ago was forced to stumble with my family through an eighteen month similar struggle with cancer that ended in the death of my precious daughter Suzanne at age twenty-three. This honest memoir is a reminder to me and to all of us who will take the time to read it that God's faithfulness is not just evident in times of physical and material abundance. It is a constant even in the darkest night, those moments of greatest physical pain and frightening uncertainty about the future. What a testimony this is of God's presence "through it all."

—**John Huffman**
Retired Presbyterian pastor and former
Chair of the Board of World Vision
Currently serving as "Minister-at-Large" and
Chair of the Board of Christianity Today and
Gordon-Conwell Theological Seminary

There is no doubt about the fact that the Lord himself intervened dramatically in answer to many prayers in the case of Daniel Schlueter. As Dan retraced his steps during those days of pain and anxiety in the pages of *In the Crucible: How God Sustains and Transforms in Hard Times*, the drama of events and the experience of waiting on God day by day and week by week are played out on these pages to the glory of God. This book will be a source of enormous encouragement to all who must walk through similar dark days in their own lives. Therefore, it is a joy to commend this work to all who must travel the same path and who long to have the same companionship of a Lord who walks with them and who never leaves them alone.

—Walter C. Kaiser, Jr.
President Emeritus
Gordon-Conwell Theological Seminary

There are few life experiences that test a person's faith and resolve more than when they learn that they or their loved one has cancer. We are often left questioning our beliefs, our past decisions, and our future. The confusion, sadness, and anger that arise from learning one's diagnosis can often lead people astray. But it is also in these dark and lonely moments that we have the opportunity to renew our faith and find a deeper love. Dan's personal story is an inspirational read. It reveals the abundant grace and love of a Father who never forsakes us. Dan's faith and uplifting attitude is as important as any treatment he received, perhaps ultimately more so. Walking with Dan through his journey, we have the opportunity to reaffirm our love and faith as we share his trials, and though we do not know the future, we can embrace it in the strength and knowledge in our Lord.

—Jon O. Wee, MD
Co-Director of Minimally Invasive Thoracic Surgery
Brigham and Women's Hospital, Boston, Massachusetts
Instructor, Harvard Medical School, Boston, Massachusetts

In this transparent account of his and his wife, Lita's, journey through one-and-a-half years of cancer diagnosis and treatment, Dan Schlueter has given us an inspiring testimony to the transforming power of God in the midst of one of the most challenging of life's experiences. Included in this account are the e-mails that Dan periodically sent to his praying friends and family, documenting his treatment and also his personal reflections and what he was learning from God during his ordeal.

This personal journey promises to be a great encouragement to all of us who find ourselves in one of life's "crucible" trials. From his own experience, Dan testifies to the fact that God is present in all of life, and is able to use everything we go through to transform us into His likeness.

A book to be cherished and passed on!

—Joanna Mockler
A friend and prayer supporter
Past Chair of Board, World Vision-U.S.

Every day Christians around the world witness to their faith in the face of deadly disease, personal and social tragedy, and religious persecution. For them spiritual war is constant and perennial. And God's grace is their only hope. Dan Schlueter's *In the Crucible* is a life-changing testimony of the power of God's grace. And it will be used by God to encourage and strengthen believers around the globe and to open non-believers' eyes to the unfailing love of God.

—Kevin Xiyi Yao. Th. D
Associate Professor of World Christianity
and Asian Studies
Director of Mission Program
Gordon-Conwell Theological Seminary

To read *In the Crucible* is to be on an incredible journey with Dan, Lita, and the Lord. Friends throughout the world anxiously awaited "postcards" from the travelers, eager and hopeful that each of the intended stops on the journey would happen as planned; that Dan and Lita would be physically, emotionally, and spiritually cared for along the way.

I was one of those people hoping for "postcards." Postcards telling of wonderful things seen on the journey, new experiences, interesting people, strange "nutrition," contacts with family and friends. The "postcards" came in the form of e-mails. E-mails written with transparency. Explanations of science and medicine. New learnings. Insights. E-mails that made one think, ponder, cry, pray, reach-out. E-mails putting oneself in Dan's shoes, wondering how I would handle being "in the crucible?" Or, how about in Lita's place?

Dan and Lita's journey is one some readers will have taken. Others will right away see a parallel time in their life or the life of a friend, a neighbor, a colleague or member of their family.

Most of us hope never to have to view the things seen on Dan's journey. They came in required stops along the way. "Passport control" you might say. Readings of x-rays and scans in the course of chemo and radiation and at the completion of treatment. Wonderful? Yes. For Dan they showed progress—"passport control" to the next stop. At the conclusion a big "Thank You, Lord!" cheers, high-fives celebrations. New experiences? Yes, with each health care facility, each new medical practitioner, each new technician and other healthcare professional, each test, each day's procedure. More new experiences than any of us would choose to have! Interesting people? Everywhere. Dan and Lita became family to them and they in turn were cared for by Dan and Lita. The conclusion of Dan's treatment equaled the continuation of these relationships. Dan and Lita's prayer list has only become longer as a result of Dan's journey!

I clearly remember hearing Dan's diagnosis. I was not a beacon of hope that day. Having a bit of medical knowledge, I knew the diagnosis was not good. With hundreds, maybe thousands, of Dan and Lita's friends, I began praying . . . and seeking updates.

Rays of hope and thanksgiving came with Dan's e-mails. Intervals. Waiting. Praying. Waiting some more. Being in the crucible. Now, you get to read Dan's e-mails!

Such a difference it was for me reading those e-mails over the course of Dan's treatments, surgery, and recovery . . . and then reading them at one sitting! Yes, by hours on the clock, the journey was shorter . . . but Dan's writing doesn't let you miss an hour of being in the crucible. Each chapter has an e-mail that Dan has enhanced with the perfect title, simple (memorable) scripture and prayer.

Throughout the book, my list grew as to who needed to read it, to whom I needed to gift a copy. For all those in the crucible . . . and for all of your friends in the crucible, Dan's book . . . slowly read; rapidly read . . . it's a gift.

—Joyce Godwin
Retired healthcare executive and corporate director
Past chair of several national and international ministries
and community leadership organizations

Contents

Acknowledgments

FROM THE VERY beginning, after just a few of the reflections contained herein were written, my older brother, Dave, strongly encouraged me to have them published. Then Yousef Sarkes from Egypt told me, "Dan, you need to publish your reflections. When you do, I will have them translated into Arabic. The Arabic Christians are too influenced by the prosperity Gospel. They need this kind of book to understand how God works even in the hard times." Thank you, Dave and Yousef, for spurring me on.

I want to thank Our Savior Lutheran Church in Topsfield, Massachusetts—they are true prayer warriors. They walked with my wife and me through a tough time. Their love for us overwhelmed and sustained us. They surrounded us, hugged us, prayed for us, and cried with us through uncertain times. They are a true testimony to the strength Christ's body provides.

I am eternally grateful to the entire Gordon-Conwell Theological Seminary community: faculty, staff, trustees, and students for their love, faithful prayers, support, and encouragement to both me and my wife. They provided rock solid support to keep us from wavering.

Thanks also go to the several hundred on our e-mail lists who received my reflections and faithfully lifted us up in prayer. Their e-mails, letters, e-hugs, and phone calls always came at just the right time to encourage us.

How can one express thanks to parents who exemplify what life in Jesus looks like? They have always prayed "specifically" for their sons and their sons' families. Arnold and Helen Schlueter, even though well advanced in years, 92 and 89, respectively, are amazing. Imagine the reaction from my three primary doctors when they received a personal letter from my parents thanking them and their staffs for taking care of their son. They love Jesus so much and that love sustained them as they remained far away from a son who was going through a crucible experience. Dad and Mom, thank you for your model of what it means to trust Jesus in every circumstance!

Finally, my entire crucible experience and this book have been uplifted by the prayers and the unceasing encouragement and love of my wonderful wife and partner in ministry, Lita. You get just a glimpse of her love and trust in the Lord Jesus Christ as you read her reflections in one of the chapters. *Muchísimas gracias mi Chula!* (Many thanks, my honey!)

—**Daniel Schlueter**
Danvers, Massachusetts

The crucible is for silver, and the furnace is for gold,
and the LORD tests hearts.

Proverbs 17:3

Foreword

THERE ARE BOOKS about suffering that are guesses or abstractions. This book, however, is different because it is written out of the pain, confusion, and questions that arise when life takes a nasty, unexpected turn. Dan and Lita have written this book a page at a time. They have gone through an encounter with cancer without knowing how their story will end. Yet, they demonstrate what trust looks like a day at a time when we can't figure out what God is doing.

I do not know where you are in your life experience, but I do know that you will find a cane here that will help you keep your balance when you wonder how you can continue, when you have been forced to deal with "fruit basket upset" in the living of your days.

—Haddon Robinson
Harold John Ockenga Distinguished Professor of
Preaching Emeritus
Gordon-Conwell Theological Seminary

Introduction

I T IS ONE of those life experiences that crush the spirit. It is the kind of circumstance that overwhelms the emotions, makes the mind spin, weakens the body to point of collapse, and causes one to cry out, "Oh Lord, I don't know if I can deal with this." Have you ever had one of those experiences or know someone who has? Then this book is for you—read on!

Maybe your home was damaged in a devastating storm or you have relatives who just lost their home in a tornado. You might be supporting a couple who is challenged rearing a child with severe physical limitations. Your neighbor just received word that her sister was tragically killed during a family dispute. Perhaps you are a pastor who is ministering to a member who unexpectedly is at death's door and the family is in shock. Are you supporting a friend whose work environment is pushing him or her to the limit? Maybe you just received word from your doctor, "I am so sorry, but the tumor is cancerous."

An image that helps us understand how such life situations touch our entire being is that of a crucible. A crucible is a vessel that can withstand very high temperatures—temperatures that are needed for melting metal without affecting the essence of the metal itself. The thought of being in a crucible can be fearful; so how does such an image help? Peter wrote that we go through various trials, all kinds of life experiences, "so that the tested genuineness of your faith—more precious than gold that perishes though it is tested by fire—may be found to result in praise and glory and honor at the revelation of Jesus Christ" (1 Pet. 1:7 ESV). The Greek word that is translated "tested" has the meaning of "tried as metals by fire and thus purified." This is what is accomplished in a crucible—a purification, a removing of the impurities. God uses the trials in our lives to bring about a transformation or a spiritual formation in our lives. He uses the crucibles of our lives to purify us, to test our faith—but always for His glory.

This image is used a number of times in scripture. In Deuteronomy 4:20 we read how the Lord considers the time the Hebrews were in Egypt as being in an iron-smelting furnace. In Proverbs we read: "The crucible is for silver, and the furnace is for gold and the LORD tests hearts" (Prov. 17:3). Isaiah writes: "Behold, I have refined you, but not as silver; I have tried you in the furnace of affliction (Isa. 48:10).

But amazingly we are not alone in the crucible. The most vivid example is that of Shadrach, Meshach, and Abednego being thrown into the fiery furnace—a furnace so hot that those who threw them in were killed. They were joined by a fourth man like the son of the gods, who kept the fire from touching them (see Dan. 3:25). And Daniel, when thrown into the lion's den, proclaimed that God had sent His angel to close the mouths of the lions (see Dan. 6:22).

Likewise, David observed in Psalm 23 that when he was walking through the valley of the shadow of death, the Lord did not remove him from the valley or his crucible, but He was with him in the midst of it. Do we see Him there with us? Do we recognize that He is doing something in our lives in the midst of the fire? When we do, we see the spiritually transforming work being done to form us into the image of His Son. Our relationship with the Lord is not static. He is and will always be about changing and forming us. It is easy to be so fixated on the big picture of our experience that we fail to see God present and working in even the smallest of details of our crucible experiences of life. But when we do, He gives us steadfast hearts that sustains us and we get a glimpse of how He is transforming us. As others observe our response while we are in the crucible, we become powerful witnesses of how God is present and is accomplishing His spiritual transforming work in their crucible experiences as well. Such was the case in my life.

There is something about hearing the words, "You have cancer," that takes one's breath away. It was late on a Saturday evening in March 2012 after an endoscopic procedure when word was first given to my wife, Lita, that I had esophageal cancer. The doctor thought that a bleeding ulcer was the reason behind my blood counts continuing to drop. An emergency procedure was performed to locate and stop the bleeding. Needless to say, Lita was stunned with the news that it was not a bleeding ulcer, but cancer. Being heavily sedated, I did not find out until the next morning. When the reality set in that the cancer was a tough one, with only a fifty to sixty percent survival rate in the first five years, the truth that God was with me, with both of us, sustained us. The psalmist declared, "He is not afraid of bad news; his heart is firm, trusting in the Lord" (Ps. 112:7). During the evenings of hugs and tears we acknowledged His presence and trusted Him. He gave both of us steadfast, firm hearts to persevere in the power of His Spirit for whatever lay ahead.

One of the ways that the reality of God's presence is realized in one's life is by asking people to pray, experiencing those prayers being answered, and then letting those who prayed know that their prayers were answered. Hence, we asked our respective immediate families to pray. We asked God's people at our church, Our Savior Lutheran Church in Topsfield, Massachusetts, to stand with us before God's throne seeking His grace and mercy. We asked God's people at Gordon-Conwell Theological Seminary, where Lita serves as the Dean of Students, to intercede for us before the Father. We asked many other friends, who live literally around the world, to pray for us. And God answered their prayers in mighty ways! His presence was felt and "seen" through the six weeks of simultaneous radiation and chemo, during the six-plus-hour surgery to remove my esophagus and restructure my stomach to function as both an esophagus and a stomach. His presence never left us while I was on a feeding tube for six weeks and during the months that followed while my body healed.

Because not all of our family is familiar with the use of social media tools, such as Facebook, we decided that a series of e-mails would be the best way to keep our loved ones and friends informed of my journey, and let them know how they could pray. But the e-mails turned out to be more than just information and prayer requests. As an engineer by training, I shared specifics of my treatments and how I saw God doing His transforming work in my life as a result of being in the crucible. He revealed more of Himself in the smallest of the details of my experience, and as a result many encouraged me to share those thoughts and reflections with others. This book is the result. Each section contains a word from the Lord and an e-mail which journals details and personal reflections. This is followed by additional reflections made after looking back over the past year. The section concludes with a prayer. The prayer begins with the words that Jesus used in Garden of Gethsemane as He faced His crucible experience on the Cross. They are words that express the intimacy we have with the One who loves us: Abba, Father (see Mark 14:36).

Lita and I gave great thanks to God that the first CT scan I had at the six-month mark and the second one at the year mark were completely clear of cancer. But we also know that the journey is not over. I will have more checkups and more scans. We also knew that even if the first or second CT scan had not been clear, or if cancer were to show up in the future, the truth is that God is with me and her, and we trust He will continue to provide us with steadfast hearts for the journey which lies before us! For we know that the joy of Immanuel, God with us, is our strength (see Neh. 8:10)! May He be yours as well as you are transformed in the crucible of your life, and are strengthened by a steadfast heart.

CHAPTER 1

Steadfast Hearts

A Word from the Lord

My heart is steadfast, O God,
my heart is steadfast!
I will sing and make melody!
—Psalm 57:7

Personal Reflections

March 28, 2012

Dear family and friends,

On Saturday morning, March 10, Dan went to the ER with what we thought was some kind of heart issue. Doctors discovered that he was anemic. After further testing it was thought he might have a bleeding ulcer. An emergency endoscopic procedure revealed that it was not an ulcer, but a lesion at the base of his esophagus. The pathology report on the biopsies taken confirmed that Dan had esophageal cancer (adenocarcinoma). An endoscopic ultra sound was performed a few days later

1

on Thursday, March 15. The cancer was classified as stage two with one area that might be stage three.

We met with a surgeon, Dr. Jon Wee, from Brigham and Women's in Boston on Thursday, March 22. He will be performing a minimally invasive surgical procedure which will last for six to seven hours. The procedure will involve removing most of Dan's esophagus and then elongating the stomach and reattaching it to the remaining portion of the esophagus. This will happen after Dan first getting six weeks of chemo/radiation treatments which will occur concurrently. He told us that although this is a tough cancer with which to deal, because of Dan's overall very good physical health, we "have a good chance of getting control of this."

After having a PET scan on Tuesday, March 27, we met with an oncologist at the Dana Farber Cancer Institute in Boston. The oncologist informed us that the cancer had not spread to any other parts of the body—PRAISE THE LORD! He also shared his recommendations for the pre-surgery chemo/radiation treatments. As we weighed the stress of daily trips into Boston for treatments, we decided to use an oncologist, Dr. "Sandy" McIntyre and a radiologist, Dr. Walter Sall, who are both within ten minutes of our house.

How can you pray for us?

First, in Mel Gibson's movie, *The Passion of the Christ*, as Jesus is about to be scourged, He prays, "My heart is ready, Father. My heart is ready" (see Ps. 57:7). Pray that no matter what we experience, what news we hear, what pain we experience, that our hearts will be ready! Pray that our hearts will be steadfast.

Second, we live in New England and all of our family lives west of the Mississippi. It is at times like this that it would be wonderful to be close to family. Thankfully, phone calls, e-mails, and even Skype, keep us well connected, but it is still difficult. Please pray that our family will experience God's grace and peace in the days ahead.

Martin Luther wrote in his commentary on Psalm 118:5 that experiences like we are going through allow us to see another aspect of God's person and they help us grow accustomed to doing battle with Satan and sin, and that by God's grace we will be victorious. Please know that each prayer that you lift up adds more and more to the Lord's army which is surrounding both of us for the battle that lies ahead. Each prayer helps us keep our eyes on Jesus and on living for Him today. Each prayer helps us remember that we can trust Him for what lies ahead each day, week, month, and year. Thank you for standing with us before the throne of grace!

Love and blessings,

Dan and Lita

Upon Further Reflection

None of us wants to go through hard experiences, but *how* we go through them will greatly shape our spiritual formation. Asking "Why me?" is very natural, but it is much more transformative to ask "to what end?" Asking the Lord to teach us, to mold us, to know more of Him, to give us steadfast hearts in the hard times—in the crucible of life—is an acknowledgment of our need to trust Him to see us through to the end.

Paul wrote to the Galatians that it was some ailment that resulted in the Galatians hearing the Gospel (see Gal. 4:13). Is it any wonder then that he wrote to the believers in Corinth that wherever we are, whatever we are experiencing, we are the fragrance of the knowledge of Christ. We are the aroma of Christ to all (see 2 Cor. 2:14-15). My crucible experience placed me in contact with people whom I would otherwise probably never have met. It provided the opportunity to share with all, some Christians and some not, the truth of the good news of Jesus Christ. This led me to start a prayer list of everyone who was involved in my care: doctors, nurses, technicians, therapists, receptionists, and custodial workers—a list, which I still pray through to this day. As I prayed I realized that it affected how I talked with them, how I related to them, how I could encourage them, how I would see the Lord in the smallest of details through what each of them performed in caring for me and how I expressed my thanksgiving to them.

Are you going through such a time as this? Do you know someone who is? Look for Him in the details—He is there! You too will be, as I was, amazed as He reveals Himself in the smallest of details.

A Prayer

Abba, Father, when the going gets tough, thank you for providing me with a steadfast heart. Thank you for letting me see You with me in the smallest of details. Thank you for allowing me to be the aroma of Christ in the presence of all with whom I come in contact.

CHAPTER 2

Prayers Keep Us Focused

A WORD FROM THE LORD

Rejoice with those who rejoice, weep with those who weep.
—Romans 12:15

PERSONAL REFLECTIONS

APRIL 4, 2012

Dear family and friends,

After meeting yesterday (April 3) with the radiologist, Dr. Walter Sall, the schedule for my treatments has been set.

I will start my chemo radiation treatments next Tuesday (April 10). Although the chemo will aid in fighting cancer, the chemicals (carboplatin and paclitaxel) are primarily given to make the radiation more effective. I will receive the chemo treatments weekly each Tuesday and the radiation five days a week for five-and-a-half weeks (28 days total). This means that treatment will end on May 17. Depending on my recovery from the effects of the treatment, surgery will occur sometime in mid to late June.

Lita and I received training on the chemo procedure. It will take about three hours and will include extra meds to aid with the flow of the chemicals and to ward off nausea. We marvel at how God has endowed the medical community with knowledge. The radiation procedure I will receive is known as IMRT (Intensity-Modulated Radiation Therapy). The intensity of each beamlet is controlled very precisely. The shape of the beam changes hundreds of times during each treatment. As a result, the radiation dose *bends* around important healthy tissues in a way that is impossible with other techniques.

I have been told to put on as much weight as possible! As I go through these two treatments it is expected that I will lose about 10 pounds or more—so I have been given the green light to enjoy milkshakes! They want the weight loss to come from fat not muscle. They want me to be as strong as possible for the follow-up surgery.

Thank you for all of your prayers and kind greetings. They keep Lita and I focused on Jesus each day, and that keeps our hearts strong for the journey ahead.

Love and blessings,

Dan and Lita

Upon Further Reflection

Do others know of the burdens you are carrying? Do they know about hard days at work? Does anyone know the weight you are bearing as you care for your elderly parents? How many know of a risky surgery you are facing? Asking people to pray brings a reality to the Lord's command that we "Rejoice with those who rejoice, weep with those who weep." It is understandable that when others know of the burdens that you carry, you might be overwhelmed by conversations and questions. You might even be wondering if others will question your faith. But Proverbs 18:1 challenges us when we might consider isolating ourselves: "Whoever isolates himself seeks his own desire; he breaks out against all sound judgment." Although there may be times when privacy is desired and good, when you ask others to pray for you, it allows His body to work the way He designed it and will result in a steadfastness of heart and will gladden the Father's heart.

There were two special times we were awed by how God was moving in His body. Imagine the tears that came to our eyes when we heard from a nephew and his wife about how their children, Amare, Miguel, and Liam, who were six, four, and two, respectively, at the time, would pray for me during their dinner prayers each evening. If they inadvertently forgot to pray for me, Miguel would pray. "And be with Uncle Dan to make him feel better." The Father's heart must have been thrilled. Then there was the new international student who, after having been under house arrest in Asia for two years for his faith, was granted permission to study at Gordon-Conwell. When he was introduced to my wife he asked, "How is your husband?" When she asked him what he meant, he told her that he had received word that I had cancer and he had been praying for me. When we heard this we were both moved to tears. When you hear how God is moving His children to pray for you, your heart will be encouraged. When others hear of how God is strengthening your heart to endure, they will be encouraged in their crucible experiences.

A Prayer

Abba, Father, thank you for hearing the prayers of your children that help me keep my focus on You, especially during those hard times in my life. May my sharing with others about how you are keeping me focused on You encourage them as well.

CHAPTER 3

God's Gift to the Medical Community

A WORD FROM THE LORD

Trust in the LORD with all your heart,
and do not lean on your own understanding.
In all your ways acknowledge him,
and he will make straight your paths.
                                    —Proverbs 3:5,6

PERSONAL REFLECTIONS

APRIL 11, 2012

Dear family and friends,

Thank you so much for all the cards, e-cards, and e-mails, but most of all for your prayers. Lita and I are deeply aware of God's grace in our lives through your powerful prayers. It is because of your prayers that we both keep focused on Jesus and living for Him TODAY!

I had my first radiation and chemo treatments yesterday, Tuesday (April 10), and both went very well.

Your prayers were specifically answered in regards to my chemo treatment. One of the chemicals, paclitaxel, can cause allergic reactions and cause the blood pressure to drop. Because of your prayers, neither of those occurred which means I can continue with treatments as planned. The chemo treatment ended up taking three-and –a-half hours so it was wonderful to have Lita with me. She was able to do her work remotely while I read and listened to music on my new iPod Nano—a gift from the small group we belong to at our church! The only significant side effect was because of the steroid product they gave me—I didn't sleep a wink last night! The steroid helps counter any reactions to the chemo and helps with the flow of the chemo, both of which are worth the side effect. Another side effect of the steroid is a flushed face. Both of these should diminish today.

Your prayers were also answered in another incredible way. Today I had my second radiation treatment and was again made aware of how God has gifted the medical community. My radiologist started using a procedure which cuts down on the setup time and increases the precision of the treatment even more. It is called Image Guided Radiation Therapy (IGRT). Once I am situated for the treatment, two x-ray machines which are mounted in the ceiling take images of my body and send them to the treatment machine which then aligns my body precisely for the treatment. This technology has only become available in the last several years, and the machine they are using for me is the best in the world—it targets cancer cells to within one millimeter!

In a devotional that Lita and I read this morning, we were reminded of how God is the One who created time and that we need to live within its limits, trusting Him for this day and not becoming anxious about tomorrow—He is forever in our presence.

That is our prayer as we walk this journey. Thank you for walking it with us.

Love and blessings,

Dan and Lita

Upon Further Reflection

As wonderful as modern technology is, that is not where we place our ultimate trust. Although technology, such as IGRT can target the radiation beam to within one millimeter, trusting the One who is actually controlling the beam helps bear the weight of the burden of any treatment. This is especially important when we realize that not everyone who requires radiation treatments has access to the latest technology. If our trust is in the technology, then those who live in parts of the world where such technology is not available would have no hope. It is when we completely trust Him that our hearts remain steadfast. A paraphrase of Proverbs 3:5-6 might be: Trust in the Lord with all your heart and lean not on the technology. In all your ways acknowledge Him and He will direct its use on your behalf.

A Prayer

Abba, Father, thank you for being the one who controls any treatments received. May I put my complete trust in You. May you help me to live in Your presence each day!

CHAPTER 4

Healing by Light

A WORD FROM THE LORD

And God said, "Let there be light,"
and there was light.

—Genesis 1:3

Again Jesus spoke to them, saying,
I am the light of the world.

—John 8:12

PERSONAL REFLECTIONS

APRIL 18, 2012

Dear family and friends,

THANK YOU FOR YOUR PRAYERS. The results from my blood work showed that I was normal in all categories. As a result I was able to have my second chemo treatment yesterday, and again the Lord was good in keeping my body from any kind of allergic reactions to any of the chemicals. There have been no major side effects to the chemo so far. I am a bit fatigued, but quick naps perk me right up. Insomnia again was the major side effect of the steroid they gave me, but I trust that, as was true last week, it will only last one night.

THANK YOU FOR YOUR PRAYERS. I had my seventh radiation treatment this morning and then met with the radiologist. He is *very* pleased with my progress. I have also been able to keep my weight in check but it requires that I consume about 3,500 calories a day—wow that is a lot! He also confirmed that my blood tests showed everything as normal which means my immune system is still normal! Thank you, Jesus! He told me that I have the strongest overall health of anyone the clinic has seen with esophageal cancer! Thank you, Jesus!

THANK YOU FOR YOUR PRAYERS. I learned in talking with the radiation therapists who perform my treatments that I am NOT receiving any kind of radioactive dosage. I am being treated with photons. Photons are bundles of energy that we call light, which are always in motion. Depending on the amount of energy a photon has, it will either behave like a wave or a particle. The lowest energy photons are known as radio waves (radio and TVs with antennae use these). Next are cell phone waves (for all our smart phones), then microwaves (for heating food and telecommunications) and finally infrared (for your TV remote). All of these light waves are invisible to the eye. Next in line in energy is visible light. All the colors of the rainbow are just the right balance between photons acting like a wave and a particle. As the energy of the photons increases, they become more like particles and we get ultraviolet rays, those nasty rays that cause sunburn. Next are x-rays; these are most commonly used by doctors to see the inside of our bodies. These are the photons I am receiving, but they are given to me at a much higher dosage level.

Imagine that—light is being used to heal me. The first thing God spoke into being was light (see Gen. 1:3)! The first thing He created was photons! Then consider that Jesus declared, "I am the light of the world" (John 8:12). As I lie on the treatment table and receive the treatments from six different angles, I visualize Jesus as the light of the world standing right there with me, reaching His finger in and weaving His finger around the good tissue while touching the cancer cells to destroy them and bring His healing!! What an awesome God!! He is indeed the Great Physician.

Lita and I are so blessed to have all of you faithfully going into the very throne room of God on our behalf. His incredible peace sustains us each day! "Give thanks to the Lord, for He is good, for His steadfast love endures forever" (Ps. 136:1).

Love and blessings,

Dan and Lita

Upon Further Reflection

Lita and I are blessed to belong to a small group at our church that walked closely with us on our spiritual transforming journey. They literally walked their talk by participating in an esophageal cancer walk. One of the members in our group designed a T-shirt for all of us. We were known as 'The Photons, Those Healed by the Light!'

Not going it alone is made very clear in a survey of the "one another" passages in the New Testament. We are to "love one another," "be devoted to one another," "honor one another," and "live in harmony with one another." There is the need to "accept one another," "greet one another," and "wait for each another." As we are a part of the body of Christ we are to "have equal concern for each another," "serve one another," "bear with one another," and "be kind and compassionate to one another." In our worship we are to "speak to one another in psalms, hymns, and spiritual songs." In humility we are to consider others better than our self. As we live for Christ there is always the need to "encourage one another and build each other up" and "spur one another on." To maintain unity we need to "confess your sins to each other and pray for each other" and "offer hospitality to one another." How wonderful to belong to a group where these traits are experienced—especially when going through hard times in a crucible. We need others to walk with us to keep our hearts steadfast.

A PRAYER

Abba, Father, thank you for healing me in all ways by the Light. May you bring others around me that will encourage me and build me up in my walk with You.

CHAPTER 5

A Wonderful Sleepless Night

A Word from the Lord

I lift up my eyes to the hills.
From where does my help come?
My help comes from the LORD,
who made heaven and earth.
He will not let your foot be moved;
he who keeps you will not slumber.
Behold, he who keeps Israel
will neither slumber nor sleep.
—Psalm 121:1-4

Personal Reflections

April 25, 2012

Dear family and friends,

THANK YOU. Lita and I continue to be overwhelmed at all of the prayers that are being lifted up on behalf of both of us. We are truly blessed to have so many interceding on our behalf before the Father. He is answering your prayers in ways that are beyond our understanding. Thank you also for the continuing stream of cards and e-mails that are always so timely. God is so good!

PLEASED WITH PROGRESS. After having my third chemo treatment yesterday (Tuesday, April 24), I am now halfway through my chemo treatments. I had my 12th radiation treatment this morning and will be halfway through those treatments on Friday. We met with my oncologist yesterday and my radiologist today and both are very pleased with my progress. Although my white blood cell count is lower, which is to be expected, it is still in the acceptable range. I have been able to put on about six pounds which is very good. They want me to continue to add weight because of what I will lose as a result of my surgery. The fatigue factor is starting to increase, and I do have some redness at the center of my back which the radiologist classified as grade one (very low).

A WONDEFUL SLEEPLESS NIGHT. Last night before going to sleep, knowing that insomnia would once again be experienced, Lita prayed, "Father, give my honey a wonderful sleepless night!" He answered her prayer. As I was awake in bed, I started to think about how incredibly the body's immune system works. The white blood cell count is so important. It is the heart of the immune system. Our bone marrow produces the red blood cells which carry oxygen to every part of the body. White blood cells protect the body against foreign invaders, and platelets aid in the clotting of blood. The red blood cells move fast. It takes one minute for a drop of blood to make it from the heart to the toes and back. The WBCs (white blood cells) however actually crawl along the lining of the blood vessels chemically interacting with the vessel walls. When there is something wrong, an infection, some foreign invader, a chemical reaction tells the WBCs to slow down, help is needed. Something incredible then happens; the WBCs, which are circular in shape, transform themselves into very thin structures that can penetrate the blood vessel walls. Once on the other side of the vessel walls, the WBCs transform back into the circular shape and start to eat up the invader. And so the body heals itself. Unfortunately, cancer cells are like "wolves in sheep clothing." The WBCs don't think anything is wrong and so help has to come from the outside. As I thought about this, I realized that in either case, whether my healing comes from the inside or the outside, it is still the Lord who will bring the healing.

IT'S ALL ABOUT HIM. I marveled at this. As I continued thinking on this, the Lord asked me, "Dan, don't you realize that if I heal you it will only be temporary?" I suddenly realized—yes it is only temporary. Jesus raised Lazarus from the dead, but he still died. Jesus raised Jairus' daughter, but she too later died. In Nain Jesus raised the widow's son and yes, even he died later. Then why did He raise them from the dead? Why did He heal anyone if they would still ultimately die? It all of a sudden hit me. I told the Lord, "This is not about me—this is all about You isn't it?" "Yes," He replied. When the Lord heals it causes people to praise the Lord and to give Him the glory. That is what Paul meant when he said, "For me to live is Christ and to die is gain (Phil. 1:21). I was moved to tears!

THE PERFECT WHITE BLOOD CELLS. I also thought about how, even though our bodies can heal themselves, it is only temporary because sin has infected our very DNA and there is only one kind of blood that can cure this disease! "The blood of Jesus his Son cleanses us from all sin" (1 John 1:7). John also had a vision of the great multitude standing before the throne of God. He wrote about the perfect white blood cells:

These are the ones coming out of the great tribulation. They have washed their robes and made them white in the blood of the Lamb.

18

Therefore they are before the throne of God,
and serve him day and night in his temple;
and he who sits on the throne will shelter them with
   his presence.
They shall hunger no more, neither thirst anymore;
the sun shall not strike them,
nor any scorching heat.
For the Lamb in the midst of the throne will be their
   shepherd,
and he will guide them to springs of living water,
and God will wipe away every tear from their eyes.
                                              (Rev. 7:14-17)

I was again moved to tears—the Lord had indeed given
me a wonderful sleepless night!
   May the Lord bless each one of you. May He make
His face to shine on you. May He turn His face toward
you and give you His peace (Num. 6:24-26 paraphrased).
Through your prayers this same blessing has been
answered in both of our lives.
   With all of our love,

                     Dan and Lita

Upon Further Reflection

When sleepless nights occur how wonderful it is to be
reminded that the Lord does not slumber or sleep. He is
available to talk no matter the cause of the sleeplessness.
When sleep flees during the night, it provides a time when
there will be no interruptions in your conversation with
Him. Entrust your anxious thoughts, your family, and
friends, your physical ailments, your relationships into
His care. Whatever comes to your mind while you are
awake, view it as the Lord tapping you on your shoulder,
indicating there is something He wants you to bring into
your conversation with Him. Your sleepless night can be

wonderful as well. Even then the Lord will strengthen your heart.

A Prayer

Abba, Father, thank You for never slumbering or sleeping. Thank You for taking my sleepless nights and turning them into a wonderful time of intimacy with You.

CHAPTER 6

Breathtakingly Unique

A WORD FROM THE LORD

Everyone who is called by my name,
whom I created for my glory,
whom I formed and made.

—Isaiah 43:7

PERSONAL REFLECTIONS

MAY 2, 2012

Dear family and friends,

DOING FANTASTIC! Those are the words from my radiologist this morning. He told me that the vast majority of those being treated for esophageal cancer have a very rough time when going through the treatments. He told me I am one of the rare exceptions. I told him that my wife and I attribute this to those who are praying for us literally around the world. Although my white blood count is lower, there is still no major concern about being around people. His caution: "Just be careful." The redness on my back has not changed from last week—just a very mild case. Lita applies a wonderful aloe gel every night which keeps everything in check. Fatigue is affecting me a bit more these days, but that is to be expected. My chemo treatment yesterday went well. Even though I still experienced insomnia last night, there were times that I drifted into sleep. My doctor says the fatigue factor probably played a role in my getting some sleep.

FORMED TO PERFECTION. After one of my recent radiation treatments, I talked with the radiation therapists a bit longer than normal, and when they took the sheet off the table I lie on, I noticed that the support form used for my head and arms had my name written on it. I found out that during my very first treatment, they had used a special "bean bag" support for my head and arms and that once situated, they extracted the air from the bag creating a special form just for me. Everyone treated has a unique "bean bag" support.

BREATHTAKINGLY UNIQUE. As I thought about this I could not help but think of something I had written about in my doctoral thesis. In our last trip to a theological college in North India, as a part of my studies, Lita and I had a number of opportunities to teach the students. We discovered that even though they are Christians who are ready to die for Jesus, many of them do not like who they are. As a result some have concluded that God made a mistake when He made them. We shared with them what David wrote in Psalm 139:

> For you formed my inward parts;
> you knitted me together in my mother's womb.
> I praise you, for I am fearfully and wonderfully made.
> Wonderful are your works;
> my soul knows it very well.
>
> (Ps. 139:13-14)

The meaning behind the Hebrew word for "fearfully" is "awe inspiring" or "breathtaking." The meaning behind the Hebrew word "wonderfully" is "distinctive" or "unique." The meaning behind the word "wonderful" is "marvelous" or "extraordinary." In other words, when you and I were born we took God's breath away as He witnessed His unique creation, each twist and link of the helix of the DNA molecule being exactly as He intended! He wouldn't change a thing about us—we are formed just the way He wanted us. We are marvelous! God did not make a mistake when He made us. He knew exactly where, when, and to whom we would be born. Our culture mistakenly places value on what we should look like, how smart we should be, how much money we should have. Therefore, it is easy to conclude that we are mistakes when comparing ourselves to others. We need to value what the "Creator" says about us rather than what "the creation" says. Oh, how the students were encouraged! They realized they needed to celebrate their breathtaking uniqueness because in that uniqueness God has a special purpose for them—to bring glory to Himself.

HIS WORKS ARE INDEED WONDERFUL. Our bodies are completely unique. Even identical twins have different fingerprints! My body is so unique that it took the specialists at Mass General Hospital a full week to run the simulations to develop the 3-D model of my body and then use that model to determine the exact angles to aim the photons so as to miss as much of the healthy tissue as possible. I now meditate on these things each time I lay down on the radiation table and place myself in the unique form made just for me. I pray that the Lord will give each of you the faith to believe that the next time you look in the mirror you can say to yourself: "God did not make a mistake when He made me. He made me exactly as He wanted me." You too can join me and David in praising God; for His works are indeed wonderful!

TWO SPECIAL PRAYER REQUESTS. My father always wants to know specific prayer requests. He wants his prayers to be more than, "Father, bless our children." So here are two specific requests.

First, I passed my oral exams for my doctoral thesis in January and then received the official word from Gordon-Conwell Theological Seminary on February 24 that I had completed all of the required work and would be able to graduate! Yeah! (That word came just two weeks before I was diagnosed with cancer.) Graduation is Saturday, May 12. Would you join me in asking that the Lord would give me the strength to attend! Lita has made arrangements to have a wheelchair for me just in case I'm too weak to walk.

Second, Lita, as Dean of Students of Gordon-Conwell Theological Seminary, is coordinating a senior banquet (this Friday) and all of the commencement activities (next weekend) and getting ready for the trustees' meeting next week. This week and the next are full ones for her—day and night. Please join me in asking the Father to give her the strength and peace as she carries out her responsibilities in addition to keeping a loving, watchful, caring eye on me!

We can never say too many times, thank you so much for all of your prayers—the Father loves it when His children talk to Him about His other children! Your prayers help keep us faithful in living today with our eyes on Jesus—He will take care of tomorrow!

With all of our love, with great thanksgiving,

Dan and Lita

Upon Further Reflection

Why is it so hard for us to believe that God did not make a mistake when He made us? Why is it that so much of our self-worth lies in what our culture says about us? Years ago when I was in the military and stationed at the Pentagon, a coworker of mine shared that he had a hard time viewing God as his Father. He told me of his father who demeaned him, beat him, treated him as trash—once being literally thrown into a trash can. His emotions were severely damaged, and so his concept of a father was also damaged. I asked him to describe what he would consider a good father to be like. His description was filled with words like trusting, caring, loving, supportive, and encouraging. When I told him that he had just described God, the tears flowed down his cheeks. When God says that He did not make a mistake when He made us, let us trust what He says and not what others say. When we do, our hearts remain steadfast.

A Prayer

Abba, Father, thank you for making me breathtakingly unique. Help me to define myself the way You see me and not as my family, friends or culture define me.

CHAPTER 7

Pursuing Happiness or Jesus?

A WORD FROM THE LORD

*And he [Jesus] said to all, "If anyone would
come after me, let him deny himself and take
up his cross daily and follow me."*
—Luke 9:23.

PERSONAL REFLECTIONS

MAY 9, 2012

Dear family and friends,

ANSWERED PRAYER. Last Friday night I was able
to attend the Senior Banquet that Lita so wonderfully
coordinated for all of those graduating from Gordon-
Conwell Theological Seminary. It was a wonderful time
to greet students, faculty, and staff. The Lord gave me
just enough strength to enjoy the wonderful celebration.
Thank you for your prayers.

ANSWERED PRAYER. I experienced my first techni-
cal difficulty on Monday (May 7). There were problems

with the radiation equipment and so my treatment had to be rescheduled for later in the afternoon instead of the morning. A technician was able to fix the problem. Even though you didn't know this was happening, your prayers were answered.

ANSWERED PRAYER. Lita and I met with our oncologist on Tuesday (May 8) morning and he told me that I am doing very well. A special praise report, even though my white blood cell count is low, the specific count that they look at for determining my susceptibility to infection actually improved! On top of that my red blood count improved so much, it is back in the normal range! Praise the Lord. This means that there are no medical reasons that would keep me from the graduation ceremony on Saturday! Thank you, Lord! Although I am getting more and more fatigued and experiencing several sleepless nights, both of these problems are helped by wonderful naps. The doctor is also pleased with my weight gain—I'm up around eight to nine pounds. There is one new side effect that I am experiencing—it doesn't take me as long to shave in the morning because my hair growth has slowed down! Thank you for praying.

ANSWERED PRAYER. I met with the radiologist on Wednesday morning (May 9) and he continues to be amazed at my general health. His word to me was, "Dan, whatever you are doing, keep doing." I will. Thank you for your prayers.

A PAINFUL REMINDER. In my last update I wrote how the special form in the radiation treatment room reminded me of how breathtakingly unique we have been made—we are not mistakes. But as wonderful as this is, I recently realized that the special form does create a problem. There have been times when my arms and shoulders would begin to ache terribly during the course of my treatment. I discovered that if I don't situate myself exactly in the form, then sections of the form press into my arms and shoulders and that causes them to ache. Unfortunately, once the radiation therapists have me aligned on the table, I have to lie perfectly still, no wiggling, no adjusting my position, no movement at all for about ten minutes! So now I make sure that I am set exactly in the form before they start to align me for my treatment.

OUR CULTURE'S SCHEMATICS. As I thought about how uncomfortable it becomes if I don't "fit the mold," I thought about Paul's admonition to not be conformed to the pattern of this world (Rom. 12:2). There is a single Greek word used for the phrase "conformed to the pattern." It is the root of our word "schematic," and Paul uses it to mean "to form or mold one's behavior in accordance with a particular pattern or set of standards." I realized how serious this really is. Once we are in the form, the mold, the pattern, doing anything outside of it causes pain and discomfort, and we want to return to the form to avoid the pain and discomfort. I could not help but ask, "Have we, who follow Christ, especially those in our country, become so comfortable in our culture's patterns that even if we know we should be living differently, the pain we know it will cause leads us to stay in the pattern?" And so we try to figure out how we can live in the form of our culture and at the same time live for Jesus and have His blessings.

THE PURSUIT OF HAPPINESS OR CHRIST? As I thought some more about this the Lord asked me, "Dan, do you live for Me because of what I can give you or because of who I am?" In other words, have we been pressed into a mold that lives counter to Jesus, but still expects blessings and honor and power and glory and peace and happiness and, yes, even healing because we follow Him? Have we allowed the "pursuit of happiness" to trump the "pursuit of Christ?"

TAKING UP OUR CROSS. Through the years of my doctoral studies, a question kept coming to me over and over. Why would anyone want to be spiritually formed to be like Jesus? Being like Jesus means standing against the world. It means living outside the mold. It means taking up our cross and following Him. Taking up our cross does not mean having a bad day at work, working for a mean boss, having an unruly child, not having a job, having a boring job, having a tough class in school, or even having esophageal cancer. Taking up our cross means dying to self. It means no honor, no power, no glory—everything Jesus experienced on His cross—and yet still living for Him! I have to admit, that sounds painful and it is painful. But it is exactly what He asks us to do.

Lord, please give me (and us) the grace to live totally and completely for you knowing that in doing so, You will receive the glory. In the end we will receive the glory, the honor, the power, the joy. Give us the grace and peace to live this day for you. Amen.

Lita and I continue to marvel at how all of your prayers are being answered. Thank you so much for your faithfulness in praying for us, especially for this eventful week at the seminary.

With love and thankful hearts,

Dan and Lita

Upon Further Reflection

The call to pursue happiness is relentless. It is one of our rights isn't it: life, liberty, and the pursuit of happiness? Every fiber in our natural being wants to be happy. We cannot help but think that if we are happy that our hearts will then be steadfast, that our lives will be at peace and that then all will be well with our souls. The problem is that the more we pursue happiness, the more fleeting it becomes. The book of Ecclesiastes makes this so abundantly clear: pursuing happiness is one goal that we will never reach. It is a fruitless endeavor! Only pursuing Jesus will satisfy our hearts and souls!

But doesn't Jesus want us to be happy? Yes, but not in the sense we typically understand happiness. The beatitudes in Matthew 5 are a good example of this misunderstanding. The word 'blessed' is sometimes translated or thought of as "happy." But something just doesn't sound right when we read, "Blessed or happy you are when you are poor in spirit or when you mourn, or even when you are persecuted." That's because that is not what Jesus is saying. The Greek word behind 'blessed' is *makarios*. We, unfortunately, do not have a good English equivalent. The Greeks used this word to convey the feeling one has when everything is as it should be. In other words, when we recognize that in whatever circumstance we are in, because we are the Lord's and all is as it should be—all is right with our souls—we experience *makarios*! It is not something we pursue, it is the result of our pursuit of Him!

A Prayer

Abba, Father, may my heart's desire be to pursue You and not happiness! May I experience *makarios* in every crucible experience in my life.

CHAPTER 8

Your Work Matters to God

A WORD FROM THE LORD

Whatever you do, work heartily, as for the Lord and not for men, knowing that from the Lord you will receive the inheritance as your reward. You are serving the Lord Christ.
—Colossians 3:23–24

PERSONAL REFLECTIONS

MAY 17, 2012

Dear family and friends,

A SPECIAL GRADUATION DAY. Thank you so much for all of your prayers for strength to attend graduation last Saturday (May 12). Your prayers were so powerful, and the Lord was so gracious, that I was able to attend a trustee dinner on Thursday night, the Baccalaureate service on Friday night, and the graduation ceremony on Saturday. After the graduation ceremony, Lita and I returned home to a fully decorated house to celebrate with dear loved ones from our church family. After about an hour I had to excuse myself to get a most-needed nap. Again, thank you for *standing* and *walking* with me in prayer.

A DIFFERENT PRAYER ANSWERED. Thank you for your prayers for my last chemo treatment. However, the Lord answered them in a different way. On Monday I received a call from the oncology clinic informing me that my blood levels had plunged to a level where it would be unwise to have my last chemo treatment, so it was cancelled. The very low levels also meant that contact with people needed to be kept to a minimum. When my treatments started I was told that the goal was get five chemo treatments, six if possible. I was thankful that I was able to get the five chemo treatments.

TREATMENTS ALL DONE. I had my last radiation treatment early this morning—yeah! Again your faithful prayers have sustained me through these past six weeks. Lita and I met with the radiologist yesterday. I have been having more pronounced side effects these past days. Although I have no problem swallowing but because my esophagus is inflamed, it is causing a low-grade constant pain in my lower chest area and my back. The doctor prescribed a medicine that I use just before I eat to coat and numb the esophagus. This helps somewhat to alleviate the pain when I eat. I am also much more fatigued and my appetite is waning. The doctor told me all of these should diminish over the next week or so.

NEXT STEPS. After a follow-up appointment with the oncologist next week, on May 31 I have a follow-up PET scan, after which we will meet with the surgeon. The scan is being done to make sure the cancer has not metastasized during these six weeks of treatment. Hopefully everything will be clear and the surgeon will schedule a date for my surgery which will possibly be in the mid-June time frame.

THEIR WORK MATTERS TO GOD. After thanking the radiation therapists for all of their care for me, I asked them if they enjoyed their work. They do. They enjoy meeting people. One of them told me it was better than any desk job. I told them that even though they were working for Mass General Hospital, I believed that the Lord was working through them to help bring healing to me. They greatly appreciated my comments. I realized that this morning was probably the last time I would see them and so, after handshakes and hugs, I told them that I would continue to pray for their "ministry" of healing.

YOUR WORK MATTERS TO GOD. As I thought about how the radiation therapists' work matters to God, I was reminded of the years I worked at GE. I didn't work for GE—I worked for the Lord at GE. Even though I know that the work I did helped with their bottom line, it was far more important than that. Just as I told the radiation therapists that God was using them to help me, so I believed that during the years at GE I was helping to make sure that jet engines leaving the plant were the best, the safest, the most reliable possible. Why? The engines were and are still transporting men and women who are involved in rescue operations, supporting people defending our country and are in harm's way, flying families to weddings, funerals, and vacation spots. It was GE engines that flew Lita and me three times to do ministry in India. It was GE who flew countless others who are serving the Lord around the globe. All of my work and your work matters to the Lord because the work we do is used by the Lord for Him and His glory!!

GRATEFUL HEARTS. Lita and I both have experienced incredible peace, strength, and comfort over these past weeks because of all of your faithful and powerful prayers. Our hearts are overwhelmed with thanksgiving and praise to our great God. Thank you for walking with us on this unplanned journey. We trust you will continue walking with us as we persevere on the journey before

us one day at a time with our eyes on Jesus. Because of you, our hearts are ready. Father, our hearts are ready.
With love and ever grateful hearts,

Dan and Lita

Upon Further Reflection

I don't know if she is a Christian or not, but the radiation therapist who chose a lesser paying job so she could enjoy being with people stands in contrast to our culture that celebrates success. Too often we mistakenly confuse God's promise of prosperity, blessings, and the abundant life with success and the American dream. As a result we can find ourselves working for ourselves rather than for God. A simple review of the lives of the disciples, Paul the apostle, and the early church should be enough to correct our understanding of how the Lord sees success.

A Prayer

Abba, Father, thank You for reminding me that I work for You and not for myself. May all of my work glorify You.

CHAPTER 9

Tough Days

A Word from the Lord

*When a woman is giving birth, she has sorrow because
her hour has come, but when she has delivered the baby,
she no longer remembers the anguish, for joy that a
human being has been born into the world.*
—John 16:21

Personal Reflections

May 23, 2012

Dear family and friends,

Over this past weekend the pain from the irritation
and inflammation in the esophagus became much more
intense. On Monday my radiologist prescribed a powerful
pain killer which has really improved my ability to eat
and sleep. Your prayers sustained me through some tough
days—THANK YOU!

Lita and I met with the oncologist this morning and
he is very pleased with my progress. My blood count

levels have improved, but are still very low, so I need to continue to restrict my contact with people.

I hope to send out another update after the follow-up PET scan and meeting with the surgeon next Thursday morning, May 31.

Your faithful, powerful, and effective prayers are greatly appreciated.

With love and blessings and thanksgiving,

Dan and Lita

Upon Further Reflection

Even though I was told to expect pain in the last stages of my radiation treatment, I had told myself that I was ready because I have a high threshold for pain. But I soon discovered I was wrong. A simple drink of water brought tears to my eyes because the pain was so excruciating. As I think back on those two days of intense pain, it is now just a memory. Although I know it was painful, I don't remember the pain. How good and gracious the Lord is in removing the remembrance of pain. Jesus described it in the context of the pain a woman has in giving birth to a child. She does not remember the pain because of the joy of the birth (John 16:21). The pain drives us to Him and the joy of His sustaining grace removes the memory of the pain.

A Prayer

Abba, Father, thank you for Your sustaining grace in the midst of pain, and thank You for removing the memory of the pain as we experience Your grace.

CHAPTER 10

Nothing Is Hidden

A Word from the Lord

For the word of God is living and active, sharper than any two-edged sword, piercing to the division of soul and of spirit, of joints and of marrow, and discerning the thoughts and intentions of the heart. And no creature is hidden from his sight, but all are naked and exposed to the eyes of him to whom we must give account.
—Hebrews 4:12-13

Personal Reflections

May 31, 2012

Dear family and friends,

THANK YOU JESUS! Lita and I just returned from our meeting with the surgeon, Dr. Jon Wee. He told us that the PET scan I had earlier in the morning showed that the cancer has not spread to any other organs. Although the area around the esophagus is enlarged because of the radiation, he told us that it is remarkably clear as well. As a result my surgery has been scheduled for Friday, June 22, at 7:30 A.M. Thank you so much for your prayers!

BLOOD COUNTS MUCH BETTER. I also received news yesterday that my blood count levels, although still below normal, are much improved. The white blood counts, the ones they are most concerned about, are just below the normal levels! Thank you, Lord! Thank all of you for praying that my body will continue to recover from my treatments and be as healthy as possible for surgery.

IS IGNORANCE BLISS? A PET scan involves injecting a glucose based tracer into the blood stream. After about an hour the tracer will accumulate wherever there is high metabolic activity, exactly the kind of activity characteristic of cancer cells. The tracer indirectly emits gamma rays which, when scanned, give off a glow. No glow, no cancer. It is amazing when faced with a test like the PET scan, how the potential for bad news causes the mind to debate whether or not to have the test. Isn't ignorance bliss? In other words we convince ourselves that we will be better off not knowing something, in this case, whether or not the cancer has spread. But in reality it is exactly what the doctors need to know so that whatever is discovered can be appropriately treated.

NOTHING IS HIDDEN. As I was strapped down on the platform for the PET scan, I was thinking how the scanner was piercing my body with the purpose of detecting something that if left untreated would bring death to my body. As I thought about this I could not help but think about how God's Word has that same effect. The writer to the Hebrews describes it this way: "For the word of God is living and active, sharper than any two-edged sword, piercing to the division of soul and of spirit, of joints and of marrow, and discerning the thoughts and intentions of the heart. And no creature is hidden from his sight, but all are naked and exposed to the eyes of him to whom we must give account" (Heb. 4:12-13). This is exactly what a PET scan is doing—penetrating, judging the cells, uncovering and laying bare, nothing is hidden. Is it any wonder then when confronted with the challenge to spend time with the Lord in His Word that the response might be "ignorance is bliss?" But nothing could be more harmful to our very lives than to ignore that which not only reveals those things that bring death, but also provides the very treatment that brings life. His Word brings life, spend time in it!

Our hearts are filled and overflowing with thanksgiving and praise to our wonderful God. Your continuous flow of prayers, e-mails, cards, phone calls, passages from God's Word, all come at just the right time. Lita and I continue to experience the Lord's incredible peace as we continue, one day at a time, on the journey before us. Thank you for walking with us.

Walking in His peace,

Dan and Lita

Upon Further Reflection

During a recent Ash Wednesday service, my pastor, Jefrey Jensen, reminded us of the two faces of the cross—the face of death (the wages of sin is death) and the face of life (but the gift of God is eternal life in Christ Jesus our Lord). The tendency is to focus on the face of life. But we need to look on the reality of the face of death and to look at our sin that placed Jesus on the cross. If we trivialize our sin, then we trivialize His sacrifice. If we trivialize His sacrifice, we trivialize His grace. Let us look on both faces of the cross!

A Prayer

Abba, Father, I thank You that nothing is hidden from Your sight. Thank You that Your Word that reveals also brings life!

CHAPTER 11

God's Transforming Power

A WORD FROM THE LORD

So we do not lose heart. Though our outer self is wasting away, our inner self is being renewed day by day. For this light momentary affliction is preparing for us an eternal weight of glory beyond all comparison, as we look not to the things that are seen but to the things that are unseen. For the things that are seen are transient, but the things that are unseen are eternal.
—2 Corinthians 4:16-18

PERSONAL REFLECTIONS

JUNE 21, 2012

Dear family and friends,

GET READY. I had my pre-operation exams this morning at Brigham and Women's Hospital in Boston to make sure I am physically ready for surgery tomorrow morning—all is good—I have been cleared for surgery.

I am now on a clear liquid diet for the rest of today with absolutely nothing to eat or drink after midnight tonight.

As with any surgery there is always the possibility of emergencies, etc. that can change scheduled times. We will be calling the hospital between three and four this afternoon to confirm my 7:30 A.M. time slot for tomorrow. I have to report in no later than two hours before my scheduled time which means we have to be at the hospital at 5:30 A.M.! Thankfully, we have a hotel room reserved which is about a five-minute walk from the hospital. We will send out a quick e-mail notice later today if there are any time changes.

GET SET. Lita's sister, Marylena, flew in from California on Wednesday evening to be with us for the next two weeks while I recover. This weekend is the very weekend that Lita's family was going to have the Hernandez *Legacy of Faith* reunion. Both of our families are very thankful that Marylena is able to be here to represent them. There will also be a close friend from the seminary and a couple from our small group who will wait with Lita throughout the surgery. Several folk from our small group and others are coming to our house tonight to pray for us—we are indeed blessed by the Lord Jesus through the local church.

GO! I will be undergoing what is known as the "minimally invasive Ivor Lewis esophagectomy." Wow! What a mouthful! It is a challenging six- to seven-hour procedure that has two parts. The first part involves making small incisions in the stomach area in order to restructure the stomach and make it more elongated. The second part involves turning me on my left side so that incisions can be made on my right side in order to remove all but a small section of the esophagus and then attach the elongated stomach to the remaining section of the esophagus. My surgeon, Dr. Jon Wee, has told us that I will be in the ICU for two to three days as they monitor me very closely. I can then expect to be in the hospital for another seven to eight days as they slowly wean me back onto a liquid diet. After I am released I will be on a feeding tube for six weeks to insure that I get the right nutrients until I heal to the point of being able to eat solids.

GOD'S TRANSFORMING POWER. Lita and I are amazed at how the Lord has gifted doctors to perform such intricate procedures on the human body! And although we are blessed to have a medical team with incredible gifts, it is the Giver of those gifts who grants us His peace. This past Sunday, prior to surgery, I had the opportunity to preach at our church as we await the arrival of our new pastor and his family. Reflecting on Second Corinthians 4:16 and the verses that follow, I shared with them how God has used the changes and challenges that Lita and I have gone through these past three months to renew and strengthen us day by day. Although there have been times of serious reflection and tears, His transforming power has resulted in both of us having a steadfastness of heart that we know can only come from Him. We have indeed seen other aspects of God. We have been reminded that even though I will have a "plumbing" change, it is only temporary and that the Father wants me to focus on what is unseen and eternal. What awaits all who trust in Jesus is an eternity of being in His presence. But until He comes again, as we focus on the unseen, we can be in His presence right now—and oh how that reality transforms us!

THANK YOU. We continue to lift up our thanksgivings to our great God for all He has done through each of you. Your prayers and expressions of love have ministered to our hearts.

NEXT UPDATE. Lita will send out an update as soon as possible after the surgery.

OUR PRAYER. Lord, may your hands guide Dr. Wee's hands with skill and tenderness as he operates on the one you love. Allow him to see what he needs to see, hear what he needs to hear, and if any decisions need to be made, speak to his mind according to your will. Grant strength, focus, and clarity to him and all the others who are assisting him, especially Dr. Phil Hartigan, the anesthesiologist. May Your peace fill Lita's heart as she and all the others who will be with her wait and pray. Dear Father, we ask and pray this in the powerful and precious name of Jesus Christ! Amen.

With all our love,

Dan and Lita

Upon Further Reflection

I can't see the "plumbing change" that has been made on my inside and yet I know that it has happened. We can't "see" the unseen transformation that is going on in our lives, but we know that it is happening. Focusing on the unseen is an incredible challenge. Why? Because what dominates our life is in the realm of the seen. Our senses—what we see, hear, smell, touch, and taste—are the driving influences in our life. What can help us focus on the unseen? Meditating on God's living Word does just that. Martin Luther provides a wonderful insight in his commentary on Psalm 119 that links the seen with the unseen. He writes that when we meditate on God's Word we should read it aloud. Why? Because what we see with our eyes and speak with our mouths is heard by our ears and enters our hearts. Meditating on God's living Word (see Heb. 4:12) changes our focus from the seen to the unseen.

A Prayer

Abba, Father, by the power of Your Holy Spirit give me the discipline to spend time with You in Your living Word so that my focus might change from the seen to the unseen.

CHAPTER 12

Upheld in a Wonderful Way

A Word from the Lord

Fear not, for I am with you;
be not dismayed, for I am your God;
I will strengthen you, I will help you,
I will uphold you with my righteous right hand.
—Isaiah 41:10

Personal Reflections

June 22, 2012 (An Update from Lita right after surgery)

Dear family and friends,

After six hours the doctor came out to tell me that the surgery went very well, for which we thank our merciful and loving Father!!

They moved Dan to the ICU where he is being carefully monitored.

Please pray as the medical staff works to transition him into a regular room. Also pray for wisdom as they manage his pain. He whispered to me that we should continue to pray for a "steadfast heart" as he recovers.

Thank you for your prayers. God, in His mercy, has heard them all!

In His loving hands,

Lita

June 24, 2012 (An Update from Lita)

Dear family and friends,

Good morning on a beautiful sunny day in Boston!

This weekend was when we (i.e. the Hernandez family) had planned to come together to celebrate our *Legacy of Faith* family reunion. This indeed highlights the significance of family—just as God has ordained it—loving one another! As soon as Dan is able to travel, we will go visit his parents in Fredericksburg, Texas, and then will go to College Station, Texas, for a few days.

Dan is making great progress, for which we praise the Lord! The medical staff is amazed at how well he is doing. He has already walked four times, which amazes the doctor and nurses. Walking helps prevent pneumonia.

He called his dad from the ICU the day after the surgery, and what joy with tears it brought to his dad and mom. He is an incredible loving son!

He is sleeping comfortably, only being awakened by the pain which reminds him to push the pump that releases the pain meds. The medical staff is outstanding, and they love having Dan as a patient. He is always giving them compliments and thanking them for their great care.

He will be in the ICU through today, followed by an expected seven days in what they call "a step down" room.

Thank you for your prayers on my behalf. I am sleeping well, eating healthy, and taking long walks with Marylena between our visits with Dan. The hotel where we are staying is only one-and-a-half blocks away which makes it very easy to rest while Dan himself is resting.

Thank you for your love and prayers. We are being upheld in wonderful ways.

Love and hugs,

Lita

Upon Further Reflection

When I was first moved into the ICU, I was in such intense pain that my body was shaking. Lita became concerned and asked for pain medication which took a while as the nurses waited on the doctor's OK. Two things happened that revealed how intimately present the Lord was with both of us. Because I was still coming out of the anesthesia, I do not remember the pain or asking her to pray for a steadfast heart. (See her June 22 e-mail.) I attribute my heart asking for that prayer to your prayers for me, and His moving in my heart! Second, because she was so overwhelmed at my pain, she prayed like a little child in her "mother tongue," the language her parents taught her, Spanish. How wonderful it is that when we experience such situations in our life the Lord always upholds us and gives us steadfast hearts to endure.

A Prayer

Abba, Father, thank You for Your promised presence and for always upholding us with Your righteous right hand!

CHAPTER 13

The Lord Prepares—
Reflections of a
Spouse

A WORD FROM THE LORD

An excellent wife is the crown of her husband.
—Proverbs 12:4a
An excellent wife who can find?
She is far more precious than jewels.
—Proverbs 31:10

PERSONAL REFLECTIONS

(I asked Lita, my crown and jewel, to write this chapter because, as with all crucible life experiences, they impact not only the individual, but family and friends.)

It is about 9:30 P.M. on March 10, 2012. I am in the waiting room by myself while Dan is undergoing an endoscopy. The nurses bring Dan out into the recovery room still under the effect of the anesthesia. The doctor is still not out of the surgery room, so I wait, hoping he was able to repair the bleeding ulcer. The doctor finally comes out and says, "Your husband does not have a bleeding ulcer, he has cancer." I was emotionally hijacked! All that night while lying on the recliner in his hospital room, I became overwhelmed with the fear of losing my beloved Dan. I finally fell asleep crying softly to the Father through tears that expressed my fears in a way that words could never do.

It was evident that God heard my prayer, for in the morning I woke up experiencing an incredible peace that could only come from the Father in Christ Jesus! As Dan awakened, he asked me if I had spoken to the doctor. I told him that I had, but that it would be more useful to him if the doctor spoke to him directly, since he would be able to answer any questions Dan may have regarding the procedure and the results. The doctor was at his bedside early that morning to give him the results of the endoscopy.

There was no question in my mind that I would be at Dan's side as he met with every doctor. I would take my notebook to write down everything the doctors told us, as well as make sure that all of our questions were answered. I was very aware that the peace which I had experienced that first morning after his endoscopy was still at work in my mind and heart. We were both made aware that the peace we were experiencing was evident to others when one of the doctors said, "Both of you are taking this serious matter very well." Dan replied that we had a God in whom we were trusting.

The one thing that I kept hearing in our meetings with the doctors was that it was a serious cancer with a fifty to sixty percent survival rate over five years. This reality began to press upon my heart, and once again I began to think about the frightening possibility of Dan not surviving the cancer. As I cried out to the Father, I was reminded that He had created Dan for His glory, which meant I needed to release him to the One who had created him. I knew that I could not do it on my own strength, so I cried out to the Father to please help me release Dan so that I would not be a burden to him and so that I could be the wife God desired me to be to Dan during the journey. God answered my prayer! As God enabled me to release Dan to Him, I was able to walk with him knowing that God was being glorified every step of the way, even during Dan's painful episodes. I knew that God would use Dan's suffering for His glory. Releasing him meant that I could pray without fear. I became more sensitive to the Holy Spirit about how to pray for Dan, such as praying that God would give him "a wonderful sleepless night." I became aware of how God was using Dan's reflections to minister to many people! I experienced God's sweet embrace through it all. People at work would frequently comment on how peaceful I appeared, and they marveled at how well I was able to carry on with my work in the midst of Dan's battle with cancer. It was all due to God's loving grace and mercy!

My response as a wife to Dan's cancer is based on the work of the Triune God in my life through His Word. It is He who, throughout my life's journey, has formed and shaped me in Christ Jesus, teaching me through joys and sorrows to approach life's trials and tribulations from His perspective—His eternal perspective.

My journey started with Dan on September 23, 1972, in Bryan, Texas, when I said "I do" to the man I knew God had led into my life and with whom I would walk until "death do us part." He was a gift from the Father to me, His beloved daughter. And being part of Dan's life throughout the journey, the Father lovingly and tenderly has shaped and formed me into a woman that seeks to be one after His heart.

The shaping and forming of my heart for the Father has not always been easy. It never is. However, the process has been amazing. I have been sustained by His loving grace and mercy, which have followed me all the days of my journey. He has taught me to embrace the truth that "the joy of the Lord" is my strength.

One of the truths God used to form my heart for him came early-on in my journey, shortly after I became aware that I may not be able to birth children. Like Hannah in the Old Testament, I cried out to God for a child. In God's timing, I heard His loving and tender response. Do you need children of your own in order to be fulfilled, or can I be your all-sufficiency? I created you for my glory. Can you trust Me to do it according to My purpose for you in Christ Jesus? God had prepared my heart to respond. With tears and sorrow in my heart, I confessed that I did not need my own children to be fulfilled, but that He is my all-sufficiency.

Another significant way the Father shaped and formed my heart was when He used my spiritual mentor and older brother, Mike, to speak a timely word, a few months before cancer took his life. As I sat by his hospital bed, he shared the truth of what constituted the foundation that would sustain Dan and me in a God-honoring marriage. He told me that Dan would not in his own human effort, even though he promised at the altar, be able to be faithful to that promise unless Dan "loved the Lord with all of his heart, soul, mind, and strength." For then he would know how to love me as God intended him to love me. And that I should pray for Dan, as well as for myself, so that we could live our lives as husband and wife on the journey where we would for certain encounter joys and sorrows, loving and trusting the God who brought us together. And we did pray, and God continues to answer that prayer.

A few weeks before Mike went to be with the Lord Jesus, he called me from his hospital room in Texas to relate an experience he believed I needed to hear. He so loved his little sister, that even while battling cancer, he took the time to call me. He always wanted me to know, and never to forget, that we belong to an amazing God! He had suffered terribly with cancer, but with God's amazing grace he was able to keep his eyes on the Lord

Jesus through it all. In one instance, he shared that Satan had come to him to harass him that there was no way God loved him. Satan told him that if God really loved him, he would not be suffering with cancer. And what Mike wanted me to know was that the Holy Spirit quickly brought to his remembrance what God had already said in His Word: that "nothing" can separate us from His love! So encouraged was Mike in that truth that he went around the ward and shared the Gospel with other cancer patients, staff, and doctors. Because he approached his suffering from God's perspective, even his atheist doctor came to the saving knowledge of the Lord Jesus!

God continued to shape and form me, teaching me to live life in the context of His love and from His eternal perspective. So when in 1997, I heard the words, "Lita, you have uterine cancer" I knew that God had prepared me for this journey. Nothing had taken Him by surprise regarding His beloved daughter. He assured Dan and me that we would not be walking through this valley alone. During my journey with cancer, God continued to form my heart for Him. He freed me to cry out to Him to use my suffering for His glory, and not let the enemy use it for his purposes. During my suffering, I experienced His incredible loving, intimate embrace, believing that my having cancer did not separate me from His amazing love!

And so on March 10, 2012, when I drove Dan to the emergency room, God had already prepared me for this part of my journey.

A PRAYER

Abba, Father, when I am experiencing a crucible experience in my life, may I see that it has not taken You by surprise, but that You have been shaping, forming, sustaining, teaching, and preparing my heart in all ways by Your grace and mercy so I might have a steadfast heart to endure.

CHAPTER 14

This Is Incredible

A WORD FROM THE LORD

For you have been my help,
and in the shadow of your wings I will sing for joy.
My soul clings to you;
your right hand upholds me.

—Psalm 63:7-8

PERSONAL REFLECTIONS

JUNE 24, 2012

Dear family and friends,

RECOVERY GOING WELL! Thank you so much for all of your faithful prayers for my surgery as testified in Lita's e-mail to you (see Chapter 13), and for my recovery which has gone exceedingly well. I had my first walk only seventeen hours after surgery. The nurse was only expecting me to sit in a chair, so when I stood and told her I was not dizzy or weak she said, "This is incredible." I've had a total of six walks so far and each one gets longer and longer. My vitals are also very strong. All of this is a testimony to God faithfully answering your prayers.

MOVED FROM ICU. I have been moved from the ICU and am now in a thoracic room where they specialize in caring for patients like me. As they monitor me over the next days, they will slowly start to remove the four IVs and three drainage tubes. Two of the IVs have already been removed! I will stay here for the remainder of my time in the hospital.

MEETING WITH THE SURGEON. We have a meeting scheduled sometime on Wednesday with our surgeon, and I will hopefully be allowed to begin a liquid diet. Please pray that my stomach will start to function properly so this is possible.

With thankful and loving hearts,

Dan and Lita

Upon Further Reflection

I thank the Lord that I was able to start walking so quickly. The quicker one can walk after thoracic surgery the less likely it is that pneumonia will develop. Even though I was walking, it required much assistance. A special walker was used to hold the oxygen tank and all of the drainage tubes. My natural response was to say: "I don't need any help. I can do this by myself." Nothing was further from the truth. I remember when I was stationed at the Pentagon that a coworker stated that he believed Christianity to be nothing more than a crutch. He was right. Jesus says that apart from Him we can do nothing (John 15:5). Paul reminds us that we can do all things through Christ who strengthens us (Phil. 4:13). Why is it that we feel the need to go it alone? Why do we resist acknowledging that we can't do anything apart from Christ? Is it possible that we know that if we lean on Him for everything, we will lose control of the decisions in our lives and we just don't want to give up that control? May our trust in Him be complete.

A PRAYER

Abba, Father, may my trust in You be complete. May I trust You to strengthen me for all things, knowing that as my soul clings to You, You hold my hand no matter how rough the road ahead might be.

CHAPTER 15

Amazed and Blessed

A WORD FROM THE LORD

The LORD is good,
a refuge in times of trouble.
He cares for those who trust in him.
—Nahum 1:7 (NIV)

PERSONAL REFLECTIONS

JUNE 28, 2012

Dear Family and Friends,

THIS TOO SHALL PASS. The doctors started a test run on my feeding tube on Monday evening. The purpose was to make sure that my body did not have any adverse responses. It didn't. The goal was also to test to make sure the digestive system was starting to work, that is, to make sure food would "pass through the system." That occurred at 5 A.M. on Tuesday!

SLOW RETURN TO NORMAL. Tuesday was a tiring, but active, day. My daily routine usually involves four walks—good exercise when recovering from surgery. Because the feeding tube worked, pain medications could be administered through the feeding port which is a much more effective method. The epidural I had been receiving was capped which meant the pain medication being received needed some quick adjustments to make sure my pain was controlled. It was a bit challenging in the early evening, but the adjustments were made and the epidural was completely removed at about 9:30 P.M. My catheter was then removed at about 11:30 P.M. By the end of the day I was down to two IVs, two chest drain tubes, an NG (nasal/gastrointestinal tube) tube or as I like to call it, "the nasal/gut tube" and the feeding tube. Yeah, on the way to normal—the new normal that is!

TESTING THE NEW ESOPHAGUS. Yesterday, Wednesday, was also extremely active. I received a special x-ray which involved drinking a barium drink while a real-time x-ray machine traversed the "new" esophagus and stomach to make sure there were no leaks. I passed the "swallow test" with flying colors. This meant that the nasal/gut tube and one of the chest drain tubes could be removed! This was big because it meant that for the first time since the surgery I could start to sip liquids using my new esophagus. Exhausted from the day, I crashed early for a good night's sleep.

As of right now the doctors are targeting my release date from the hospital sometime this weekend. I will receive another x-ray today (Thursday) to make sure there are no problems before they remove the final chest drain tube. The surgeon wants to make sure that my digestive system is functioning completely before releasing me.

AMAZED AND BLESSED. Pastor Jefrey Jensen, our new Pastor, visited with us on Tuesday afternoon. He shared three truths concerning the Lord that provides a testimony to His work in our lives. In Nahum 1:7, Nahum writes to a city that is being condemned and he writes how God is good, a refuge in times of trouble, and He cares for those who trust Him. Lita and I are in awe of not only what God is doing, but how fast He is doing it. We have seen these truths confirmed again and again. When we might have questioned His goodness, He showed us He is good! When we needed to run for safety, He provided the perfect shelter for refuge. At each juncture where waiting was required and we trusted Him and submitted to His timing, He responded by making our wait shorter or giving us patience as He cared for us. We know this is a result of all of your incredible and powerful prayers to our wonderful God. May the truths of God proclaimed in Nahum 1:7 be yours this day!

With ever thankful and loving hearts,

Dan and Lita

Upon Further Reflection

We might question the goodness of God when we consider all the "bad" things that happen in the world today. If God is good, then why did I get cancer? But the goodness of God must not be based on our or others' circumstances but on God's Word that very simply and without reservation declares, God is good! God is good not because of the lack of trouble in our lives, or that we are in a crucible, but because God declares it to be true. We must align our understanding of God's goodness, as well as all of His other attributes, on His Word. Our understanding cannot be based on our circumstances.

I was challenged in this area just few a days after I was transferred out of the ICU to my special thoracic room. I overheard one of the nurses ask another patient who had a surgery similar to mine how his new esophagus was working. A new esophagus? Of course the natural question to ask was, "Lord, why did he get a new esophagus and I didn't?" It is easy to call God's goodness into question when we see others receiving blessings that we think we should receive as well. But the Lord was gracious to me. Days later, just after I had been approved to begin a clear liquid diet, a nurse came and asked me, "Dan, how is your new esophagus working?" I discovered that part of my stomach acting as the esophagus is now referred by that name. Lord, thank you for keeping me from questioning your goodness in my life.

A Prayer

Abba, Father, I thank You that You are good, that You are a refuge in times of trouble and that You lovingly care for me as I place my complete trust in You.

CHAPTER 16

Held Strongly in His Grip

A Word from the Lord

The steps of a man are established by the LORD,
when he delights in his way;
though he fall, he shall not be cast headlong,
for the LORD upholds his hand.
                                        —Psalm 37:23-24

Personal Reflections

June 29, 2012

Dear Family and Friends,

We just met with the surgeon, and he is concerned that the liquids I am now taking in are not moving through my stomach fast enough. This has created a breathing problem. As a result he will be doing a fifteen- to twenty-minute endoscopy using general anesthesia later this afternoon or early evening to investigate the situation and dilate possible problem areas. This is a common occurrence for this type of surgery, but usually happens two to three weeks post-surgery. At this point my release date is uncertain.

Thank you for your faithful prayers as we wait for an operating room to open up to do the procedure.

We continue in His peace, held strongly in His grip,

Dan and Lita

Update on the June 29th procedure.

Dear Family and Friends,

Thank you very much for praying. The Lord is merciful and gracious. An operating room opened up earlier than expected. The endoscopy to dilate the stomach in the area where it empties into the small intestine went very well.

With hearts of thanksgiving,

Dan and Lita

Upon Further Reflection

Jesus told His disciples that in this world we will have trouble (see John 16:33). How we respond when we experience trouble, when we hit those bumps in the road, reveals the strength of our relationship with the Lord. If our relationship is not strong, then the tendency is to become anxious. We begin to question His goodness, His care for us, even His love for us. If we are not careful, we can become angry and possibly even bitter toward God. If, however, our relationship is strong, then our trust in Him prevails and we see His goodness, His care, His love in the midst of the trouble. In my situation, it was good that the problem was discovered before I left the hospital, because it would have meant a return trip to the hospital.

A Prayer

Abba, Father, thank You for Your promise that, when I hit bumps in the road and stumble, I will not fall, because You hold my hand.

CHAPTER 17

Patient or Patient?

A WORD FROM THE LORD

Have you not known? Have you not heard?
The LORD is the everlasting God,
the Creator of the ends of the earth.
He does not faint or grow weary;
his understanding is unsearchable.
He gives power to the faint,
and to him who has no might he increases strength.
Even youths shall faint and be weary,
and young men shall fall exhausted;
but they who wait for the LORD shall renew their
strength; they shall mount up with wings like eagles;
they shall run and not be weary;
they shall walk and not faint.
> —Isaiah 40:28–31

PERSONAL REFLECTIONS

JULY 2, 2012

Dear family and friends,

HOME SWEET HOME. It is so good to be home after having been in the hospital for ten days! I was released on Sunday afternoon. On Sunday morning when I came back to my room after a walk, I told Lita that for the first time I was hit with the "hospital smell" and knew I was ready to go home. But throughout my entire stay, Lita and I trusted the Lord for His perfect timing for my release. Even the unexpected endoscopy procedure on Friday to dilate my stomach where it enters into the small intestine was considered a small hiccup and was seen as God's continuous care covering me as you all prayed.

PATIENT OR PATIENT? As I was thinking about the "hospital smell" on Sunday morning, one of the nurses asked me if I was anxious to go home. I told her that I was, but what was more important was the doctor's assessment, and that until he told me I was ready to be released, I would wait. Her response was, "My, you are so patient." I asked her "Isn't that why I'm called a patient?" Her belly laugh was contagious. Why is it so hard to be patient? The word patient comes from the Latin word *patientem* which means "bearing or enduring without complaint." No wonder some Bible translations use the word "longsuffering" instead of "patience." Just as the Lord has provided steadfast hearts for both of us during these past months, we realize that it the same Lord who, through His Spirit, provides the power to bear or endure without complaint! Lita and I agree that when we complain it means that we do not trust the Lord, either in His plan or His timing. No wonder David wrote, "I waited patiently for the Lord; he inclined to me and heard my cry" (Ps. 40:1).

NURSE LITA. Even though I know there will be challenges over the next several weeks, nurse Lita is wonderful! Her sister, Marylena, is here until Thursday. I told her that I wanted her family to know that I rate her help as "A+"! She has been a wonderful companion and help to Lita!

SPECIFIC PRAYER REQUESTS. Please pray as I adjust to being at home and having to use a feeding tube for fourteen of the twenty-four hours each day. Although limiting, I know the Lord is using it to make sure my body receives the needed nutrition. Also, please pray for our first follow-up appointment with my surgeon on Thursday morning. We are hoping to get the pathology report at that time. Until then, we wait *patiently* on the Lord.

With steadfast hearts that are filled with love and thanksgiving,

Dan and Lita

Upon Further Reflection

During the months that followed my surgery, great healing took place, but my breathing capacity was limited because my diaphragm was still adjusting to the "new plumbing." Any activity that required more oxygen was limiting because I got winded very quickly. Waiting with patience for healing was difficult.

The sense behind the Hebrew word "wait" in Isaiah 40:31 is a twisting that produces strength. When something is twisted, the tension produces strength, which then produces endurance, which builds our character and results in hope (see Rom. 5:3-4). Our waiting is not just sitting around passing time. Waiting means our hearts are being strengthened so that you and I can expectantly put our hope in the Lord because we know that He is doing His work,

His way, in His time, which, because He loves us, has to be the very best.

In my case it was good to be reminded that the Lord does not get winded or weary. His promise to renew our strength, so that we will be able to run and not grow weary and walk and not grow faint, encourages us to wait patiently for Him.

A Prayer

Abba, Father, thank You for the promised strength and steadfast heart You will provide as I wait patiently for You to do Your transforming work in my life.

Radical Condition Requires Radical Action

For the life of a creature is in the blood, and I have given it to you to make atonement for yourselves on the altar; it is the blood that makes atonement for one's life.
—Leviticus 17:11 (NIV)

...the blood of Jesus, his Son, purifies us from all sin.
—1 John 1:7 (NIV).

PERSONAL REFLECTIONS

JULY 5, 2012

Dear family and friends,

THE CANCER HAS BEEN REMOVED! We met with my surgeon this morning and he went over the pathology report with us. He said that one of the lymph nodes which was removed showed the presence of cancer. However, he is confident that all the cancer was removed during surgery and that there will not be any need for further radiation or chemo treatments. THANK YOU, Lord Jesus! We pray that you will join us in thanking and praising the Lord for His grace and mercy in our lives.

THE HEALING CONTINUES. Being pleased with my overall healing, Dr. Wee removed the special sutures and upgraded my diet. For the next week he prescribed a soft food diet after which I will be able to cut my feeding tube regimen in half. It is so good to be able to eat more solid foods! Please pray that my body adjusts well. If it does, then I can begin to eat more regular meals. I have a follow-up appointment scheduled in four weeks and the goal is to be completely off of the feeding tube in three weeks. YEAH!

With steadfast hearts that are filled with praise, love and thanksgiving,

Dan and Lita

Upon Further Reflection

Left untreated, cancer is deadly. Having cancer puts one into a radical condition which requires radical action. I cannot imagine how I would have responded if Dr. Wee had said to me, "Well, Dan, I really didn't want to cut too deep, so I left some of the lymph nodes in." No, he knew that he had to cut deeply to remove all of the cancer. So, too, God took radical action to deal with our spiritual radical condition—having the cancer of sin. What could be more radical than sending His Son, to shed His blood, to die to bring healing from the cancer of sin?

A Prayer

Abba, Father, thank You for sending Your Son to deal with the cancer of sin in my life and then create a new heart within me.

CHAPTER 19

Lord, Don't You Care?

A Word from the Lord

Teacher, do you not care that we are perishing?
. . . He [Jesus] said to them: "Why are you so afraid?
Have you still no faith?"

—Mark 4:38,40

Personal Reflections

July 27, 2012

Dear family and friends,

OFF THE FEEDING TUBE! Yeah! I had my last feeding tube regimen this past Wednesday. I have been eating regular meals—yippee! Thank you all very much for your faithful, powerful, consistent, effective prayers. There have been days when eating was a challenge, but the Lord heard all of your prayers and my body has been slowly adjusting. I am so thankful that the Lord allowed me to reach the goal of being off the feeding tube before I meet with my surgeon next Thursday, August 2.

THE HEALING CONTINUES. At times it is hard to believe that it has been five weeks since the surgery. As my body continues to heal, I have also become more mobile. Lita's brother, Moises, and our twin nephews and godsons, Nathan and Russell, visited us this past week from Texas, and I was able to be very mobile with them, even taking a trip to Rockport, Massachusetts, to see the Atlantic and walk a short time on the beach with them. What an encouraging time!

SICK OF BEING SICK. The one challenge for me these past weeks has been weariness—sick of being sick. This is where your prayers have been most welcomed. I continue to go back to God's Word again and again to be reminded of His help and abiding presence in the midst of my weariness. It is during these times that Satan comes and asks his age old questions: "Dan, did God really say He would be with you?" and "Does He even care about you?"

LORD, DON'T YOU CARE? During one of my recent quiet times with the Lord, I was reminded of the time when Jesus was with His disciples in a boat in the middle of the Sea of Galilee at night (see Mark 4:35-41). While Jesus was sleeping, an unexpected squall came up and the boat was flooded. Jesus slept. The disciples frantically tried to manage the boat and bail at the same time. Jesus slept. They finally awoke Him and asked, "Lord, don't you care if we drown?" After He calmed the storm His response seemed a bit harsh: "Why are you so afraid? Have you still no faith?" I mean, who wouldn't be afraid in such a circumstance?

But they mistook Jesus inaction as His lack of care. Instead, Jesus wanted them to look to Him even in the midst of a life threatening situation. If He is asleep, then ALL must be well. Jesus knew that even if He slept, His Father did not!

When the unexpected storms of life hit us right between the eyes, fear grips us and it is easy to ask the question, "Lord, don't You care?" Lord, don't You care about my health? Lord, don't You care when weariness sets in? Lord, don't You care when I can't eat enough to keep my weight up?

KEEP ON BAILING. What are we to do? Keep our eyes on Jesus, remember His unfailing promises and keep on bailing, but do so with hope, not fear!

PRAYER REQUESTS. Please pray that I will be able to eat the appropriate food in the right amounts not only to maintain my weight, but also to put a bit of weight back on during this next week before meeting with the doctor. Also, pray that I will keep my eyes on Jesus during the times of weariness. Thank you even now for the work the Lord will do because of your prayers.

With steadfast hearts that are filled with praise, love, and thanksgiving,

Dan and Lita

Upon Further Reflection

Does God tell the truth? The answer might seem too obvious and yet that is exactly what we need to ask ourselves when we are weary, overwhelmed, afraid, anxious, and filled with doubts. God has given us His incredible promises which cover each of these and many more conditions in which we find ourselves. We have a choice: either God is telling the truth and we can trust Him, or He is lying and then we have every reason to ask, "Don't You care?"

A Prayer

Abba, Father, thank You that because You are the truth, I can trust You and ALL of Your promises concerning Your care of me.

CHAPTER 20

Thankful Hearts

A Word from the Lord
Give thanks to the LORD, for he is good,
for his steadfast love endures forever.
—Psalm 136:1

PERSONAL REFLECTIONS

August 3, 2012

Dear family and friends,

THE FEEDING TUBE IS OUT! We had a wonderful meeting with the surgeon yesterday (August 2). After his assessment of my medical and physical progress, he decided that even though my weight is down just a bit, it is stable enough, and the feeding port was removed! Praise the Lord! Your continued prayers for my diet are greatly appreciated as there are still days when eating is a challenge.

RESTRICTIONS REMOVED. During these past six weeks I had several restrictions: no driving and no lifting of anything heavier than ten pounds. Both of these restrictions have been lifted, although he asked me to be cautious when lifting anything heavy. He also approved my traveling, and so we are making plans to travel to Texas sometime in the fall to visit our wonderful families!

NEXT APPOINTMENT AND UPDATE. My follow-up appointment is scheduled in four months in December at which time I will have a CT scan.

THANKFUL HEARTS. We have both been sustained and renewed, and are ever thankful for the many expressions of love and concern that we have received throughout this challenging journey. Indeed, we have a merciful and faithful God!

Sustained by His loving grace,

Dan and Lita

Upon Further Reflection

In Psalm 136:1, the Hebrew word that is translated steadfast love is *hesed*. It is a word that is rich in meaning. It means, "an interaction between strength, steadfastness, mercy, and love." It implies personal involvement and commitment in relationships, that is, a love that is steadfast based on a prior relationship. Is it any wonder then that we can give thanks to a God who has this kind of love toward us! Is it any wonder that we, too, can declare, "God is good!"

A Prayer

Abba, Father, Your *hesed* toward me overwhelms me, and causes me to give You thanks in all circumstances in my life.

CHAPTER 21

God Is Faithful

A Word from the Lord
The steadfast love of the LORD never ceases;
his mercies never come to an end;
they are new every morning;
great is your faithfulness.
"The LORD is my portion," says my soul,
"therefore I will hope in him."
                          —Lamentations 3:22–24

PERSONAL REFLECTIONS

OCTOBER 2, 2012

Dear family and friends,

GETTING STRONGER. Since several of you have asked how I am doing, I decided to send out a quick update. First of all, thank you very much for your continued prayers—they are being answered!! I am getting stronger and stronger as each week goes by. I say each week because there are days when, all of sudden, I become very tired and spend most of the day resting. I mentioned this to one of my doctors during a recent follow-up appointment. He informed me that even though I am doing very well in my recovery, the surgery I underwent is the most traumatic thoracic surgery done on the body, and that it will take about six months before I start to feel good and about a year to completely heal!

MY EATING AND WEIGHT. I am slowly, but surely, starting to eat bigger and bigger meals. That's relative, of course, since my meals have been much smaller than before. But my eating has allowed my weight to stabilize without having to take any special supplements, for which I am very thankful.

BACK AT THE SEMINARY. During my doctoral studies I was spending a lot of time at the seminary doing my studies in the dining hall and having wonderful, encouraging conversations with students, faculty, and staff. I was so regular that many started to refer to the table at which I sat at as my "office." As my strength has returned, I am going to the seminary every Wednesday to attend chapel and spend time in conversation. I am only able to spend about half a day as I start to get tired right after lunch.

FORTY WONDERFUL YEARS. On September 23rd Lita and I celebrated forty wonderful years of marriage. We had been planning on a large celebration, but my cancer journey changed that a bit. We did have a joyful surprise celebration with our small group and other friends from our church! They are our family here in Massachusetts, and so it was special to celebrate with them!

A VISIT TO TEXAS. Our plans are to go to Texas the first week in November to visit our families. It has been over a year since we have seen them, and they are all as excited as we are about our visit. We look forward to our times of mutual encouragement.

GOD IS FAITHFUL. We have both marveled as to how God has demonstrated His faithfulness in our lives through this entire journey. We both have developed a much deeper sense of the Lord's presence in our lives as we have turned to Him again and again for strength, peace, and security, and as a result have experienced His abiding joy. May you all experience Him in the same way!

With all our love and blessings,

Dan and Lita

Upon Further Reflection

As I was reflecting on how God has demonstrated His faith1fulness during my journey with cancer, He asked me, "Dan, do you see Me as being faithful because your healing is going so well? Would you still consider Me as faithful even if it wasn't?" It is easy to acknowledge God's faithfulness when everything is going OK in our lives. The question we have to ask is whether we acknowledge His faithfulness when we are in the midst of trials, tribulations, heartaches, pain, and suffering—when in the crucibles. When used in the Old Testament, the Hebrew word for faithfulness implies more than just reliability or trustworthiness. It also implies strength and support. This is the sense of the word when Isaiah declares that God "will be the *stability* of your times" (Isa. 33:6).

Jeremiah reinforces the truth of God's faithfulness even as he lamented over the destruction of Jerusalem by the Babylonians. It would have been easy for Israel to question God's faithfulness as they watched the city of God being ransacked and burned. But Jeremiah boldly declares otherwise. And so, no matter what our current circumstances might be, we too can declare that God's strength, support, reliability, trustworthiness—God's faithfulness—is indeed great!

A PRAYER

Abba, Father, because Your faithfulness is great, my hope in You remains steadfast!

CHAPTER 22

Transformed in the Crucible of Life

A WORD FROM THE LORD

Not only that, but we rejoice in our sufferings, knowing that suffering produces endurance, and endurance produces character, and character produces hope, and hope does not put us to shame, because God's love has been poured into our hearts through the Holy Spirit who has been given to us.
—Romans 5:3–5

PERSONAL REFLECTIONS

DECEMBER 6, 2012

Dear family and friends,

CT SCAN ALL CLEAR! It has been four months since I last visited with my surgeon, Dr. Wee, and today I had a CT scan followed by a visit with him. My scan was completely clear—thank you, Jesus! My surgical scars have healed better than expected, and everything else regarding my weight, diet, and overall recovery are very good. According to Dr. Wee, he said," You look great!" and, "You are my model patient." My next CT scan and visit with Dr. Wee is scheduled for June 2013.

VERY THANKFUL. We are very thankful for all of your faithful prayers and support as the Lord continues to do His marvelous healing in my body.

With all our love and GREAT THANKSGIVING,

Dan and Lita

Upon Further Reflection

CT stands for "computed tomography." Tomography is a combination of two Greek words: *tomos* which means "slice" and *graphein* which mean "write." A CT scan is a 3-D image that is made from slices of our bodies. As I was reflecting on this e-mail, I was suddenly struck with the thought: "What if there was a CT scan that would reveal the image of our spiritual formation?" What would it show? What impurities would light up the images? What healing and growth would stand out? Would the condition revealed be one that shows we have been tried and healed and found not wanting? The word for "character" has this sense when Paul uses it in writing to the Romans. R. C. H. Lenski writes in his commentary on Romans 5 that when Paul is writing about something that is tried or put to the proof, he is using this in a good sense. Something tried in this manner will not be wanting. Is it any wonder then that such a condition results in hope? Such a hope is real—it is not wishful thinking. And because the hope is real, it means we will not be put to shame—our hope will be vindicated—we will not be disappointed. As we are placed in the crucible of life, the Lord sustains and does His transforming work in our lives so that one day we will stand before Him and He will say, "You look great!"

A Prayer

Abba, Father, may I know that each and every trial that You take me through will result in my spiritual formation. Give me the endurance and a steadfast heart as You do Your spiritual transforming work in my life—all to Your glory!

CHAPTER 23

Grace Extends, Thanksgiving Increases

A Word from the Lord

But we have this treasure in jars of clay, to show that the surpassing power belongs to God and not to us. We are afflicted in every way, but not crushed; perplexed, but not driven to despair; persecuted, but not forsaken; struck down, but not destroyed; always carrying in the body the death of Jesus, so that the life of Jesus may also be manifested in our bodies.
—2 Corinthians 4:7-10

For it is all for your sake, so that as grace extends to more and more people it may increase thanksgiving, to the glory of God.
—2 Corinthians 4:15

Final Reflections

Afflicted? Perplexed? Persecuted? Struck down? Carrying the death of Jesus in the body? These words surely seem to describe what it is like being in a crucible. Paul uses these words to describe what he has experienced in his ministry as he lives the life he has in Jesus in a clay pot. I don't know about you, but I would much rather be a jar of steel than a jar of clay. Would not a jar of steel be better able to withstand such assaults on our very being? But then, as Paul writes, the power would not be seen as belonging to God but to us. Others would look at us and possibly conclude that if we can get through a hard time on our own strength, then they can too. Who gets the glory? We do, not God. When we hear the Lord's word to Paul that His grace is sufficient and His power is made perfect in weakness (see 2 Cor. 12:9), then He gets the glory. When others witness His grace and power in our lives which sustains and transforms us in the crucible, the truth of who God is in Jesus Christ extends to more and more people. And when they receive the truth, it will result in more and more giving of thanks to Him because He is the One accomplishing His transforming work in our lives and He is glorified.

Finally, I commit to you a promise to hold onto when in the midst of your crucible experience—He who by His grace began a good work in you, will by that same grace bring it to completion in the day of Jesus Christ (see Phil. 1:6).

MY PRAYER FOR YOU

Abba, Father, may those who have read this book and have had their hearts encouraged, see anew how You are with them in their crucible experiences. May they acknowledge that it is Your grace and power which gives them steadfast hearts to sustain them. May they see You in the details of their hard times so they recognize Your spiritual transforming work in each and every circumstance. As You extend Your grace to them, grace that saved them and grace that sustains them, may others see and experience Your grace which results in increasing thanksgiving to You, so that You and You alone are glorified. Amen.

For more information contact:

Daniel Schlueter
C/O Advantage Books
P.O. Box 160847
Altamonte Springs, FL 32716

info@ advbooks.com

To purchase additional copies of this book or other books published
by Advantage Books call our order number at:

407-788-3110 (Book Orders Only)

or visit our bookstore website at:
www.advbookstore.com

Longwood, Florida, USA
"we bring dreams to life"™
www.advbooks.com

CPSIA information can be obtained
at www.ICGtesting.com
Printed in the USA
FFOW05n0638180314